Fragrance at your doorStep

Life-changing perspectives

Fragrance at your doorStep

Life-changing perspectives

Nitu Ramchandani

PAPER TOWNS
PUBLISHERS

PAPER TOWNS
PUBLISHERS

First published by
Papertowns Publishers
72, Vishwanath Dham Colony,
Niwaru Road, Jhotwara,
Jaipur, 302012

Fragrance at Your Doorstep

ISBN Print Book – 978-93-94670-02-0

Cover by Amit Ramchandani
amitr18x@gmail.com

Dedicated to Mirav; smallest child of my family.

Acknowledgements

Big big thank you Sam (Girdhari Patidar) for coming as a healer in my life. Thank you Ashmeet Chhabra for always staying by my side. And to my biggest supporters and well-wishers, my mom, my dad and Amit Ramchandani, a big thank you!

Thanks to all the beautiful readers who chose to read my book. And a very big thank you to my dear principal mam (Sanjeevani Dobhal) from Helen Keller Blind School, for always loving me unconditionally.

Thank you everyone at the Bookoholics and my publisher, for making my dreams come true by publishing my books. Thank you so much! You make me so happy.

Contents

What is perspective shift? Perspective shift is what you give or focus your attention and energy to. It is when we choose to look at the bright and positive side of the things so as to lessen the burden of negative circumstances. From my experiences, I can boldly say that all the problematic situations in life always have some kind of hidden blessings in them. All we need to do is look at our hardships from a different point of view. Examples include: see arguments as opinions, turn loneliness to feeling peace, and etc.

Why do we need perspective shift at all? We need it because it allows us to better our mindset. The broader our perspective, the more chances we get to understand the opportunities life keeps giving us to get closer to our dreams. Also sometimes, we need it to avoid misunderstandings in relationships, when communicating things is not possible. Sometimes, what happens is that distance doesn't allow us to convey our feelings to our loved ones exactly the way we want to. This creates problems in relations and we start assuming things on our own. Perspective shift allows us to not assume things and even if we assume them, it takes care that we can at least choose to stay positive. Our outlook and how we interpret things changes everything.

How to use pressure in a positive way

There have been times in my life when I have faced extreme pressure for certain things. There was pressure to become independent, to have good looks, to marry, to get fit, to have a perfect personality, and to learn cooking, etc. Then, one day, I came across a piece of writing which said that a diamond is just a lump of coal that did well under pressure. This quote gave me strength to realize my potential and to overcome the hurdles life kept presenting before me. It's true that we all face some kind of pressure in our lives. What's important is how we deal with it. We can always use our negative experiences as opportunities to learn some new lessons in life. Whenever you feel like everyone keeps criticizing you for things, choose to face the situation so that you can prove that you are capable enough to take the responsibility to bring about a change.

Take criticism as feedback. Whenever someone makes any comment on you, you get the power to prove a point. You get to improve accordingly and you get a chance to make the other person believe in you. That's how you can also be the change.

Replace frustration with hope

Sometimes, we get frustrated when we can't understand that why bad things happen to us. I can't even remember how many nights I have cried alone and slept with tears in my eyes. I used to get more anxious when I couldn't understand the reason behind crying (during the days of suffering from anxiety, depression and insomnia). One good thing that has always kept me going is hope; hope for better days. There is always someone out there who is going through the same kind of pain as that of ours. So, we must always remember that we are never alone in our battles.

Keep shining so that the world can know your story one day and so that you can help others from facing the same kind of hurt.

Realization about blessings

Sometimes, we complain too much for every little thing that bothers us. If we'll observe ourselves carefully, we will surely realize that we keep blaming the system for different things instead of taking responsibility. For example, if a student couldn't enter into an IIT, he'll keep complaining that the exam was too tough. What he can do instead is that he can create an environment of IIT in whichever college he gets admission in. Some goals do seem a bit difficult to achieve, but complaining and worrying cannot improve any situation in life. When we worry, we suffer more. I think every time something troubles us, we can think of all the things we are grateful of. We are blessed more than we even realize. This fact alone should be enough to be recalled in our memory every time we need to motivate ourselves to keep going in life. A small change in perspective is always helpful for our growth.

Learn lessons from all those experiences the world keeps facing and apply them to your own hardships, and see the majority of problems vanishing from your life.

How to deal with tough times

There are situations in life when it gets somewhat tough to deal with certain things. Such moments make us feel like there's no solution to our problems. Also, when there's so much competition out there, there's a continuous sense of staying ahead. This can affect our mental health in a negative way. Therefore, it's important to not lose our patience in challenging times. We must never be too stern with ourselves. Staying flexible during the growth process allows nourishment of mind, heart, body and soul in a better way.

Whenever the going gets tough, remember that you can slow down and take one moment at a time.

Stop treating yourself as a victim

Whenever I am going through a tough phase in my life, I start feeling like I should be treated in an extra nice manner. I know it's not wrong to expect a little extra care when you don't feel alright, but at the same time, we should also be aware that self-care is the best way to make our hearts feel less heavy. Also, if we simply start accepting things the way they are, there will be more self-awareness. Self-awareness makes us understand exactly where we need positive changes in our habits. These changes ultimately help to bring improvement in our lives.

As long as you'll consider yourself a victim, you won't be able to come out of your hardships. Stop waiting for someone to come and cheer you up. Cheer yourself up and always remember that shifting your perspective bit by bit can always help you to change your life if you are willing enough to make it better.

Stop behaving like a victim and see how you will have cured yourself.

Keep your vibrations (vibes) high

Once I asked my uncle about how an individual could bring a change in the lives of other people if he wishes to make a positive impact. He told me to simply keep my vibrations/vibes high. Unless we follow good values and habits, we cannot make others do so. Only when our actions are in alignment with our words, can we create a positive influence. Once we learn to live by actions, we can motivate and inspire others, too.

Keep your vibrations so strong that you can create the kind of world you think you deserve to live in.

Use challenges to build strength

I feel like life keeps pushing me into dark places, but then I think this is what is called as life. Only when there are ups and downs, can we understand the value of good things.

Challenges are simply tests that make us realize how powerful and capable we are. Once we are able to realize how much inner strength we carry inside us, we can use that strength to achieve even those things that seem impossible.

Only when you have been to a dark place, you'll know the importance of light. Discover light in places where you can't see it.

Keep going with the growth mindset

Sometimes, I feel stuck and lost, and in such situations, I cannot understand what to do further. One thing that always saves me is that I keep going with the growth mindset. What I believe is that every negative experience that happens to us has some hidden life lesson in it. We must keep focusing on the lessons and not overwhelm ourselves with emotions. What I do these days is that as soon as I observe myself flowing with my emotions, I'll interrupt my mind by thinking a positive and happy thought. This helps me to stay happy and focused.

Life always feels good when you keep going. Let no one and nothing bring you down.

Stop complaining and start celebrating

There are times in life when we feel like we don't get enough appreciation for our efforts. It seems like all our hardwork goes unnoticed. Also, when we don't find enough support for our dreams, we start complaining that nothing works in our favour. In such cases, perspective shift is the best way to save ourselves from all the negativity. If we simply allow ourselves to see good in everyone and everything, we can boost ourselves to achieve great things in life.

Never let your worth depend on other people's validation of who you are. Celebrate little progress that you keep making every-time, while marching to your destination.

Create your own happiness/sunshine

Sometimes, I feel like nothing gives me relief/peace. In such times, I try my best to stay extra patient and make sure that I can regain my calmness before pessimism tries to disturb me. Also, I explain myself that great discoveries emerge by being out of comfort zone only. We can always try practicing some art so that it can provide us relief from our feelings. As simple as writing down our thoughts can also prove to be a beneficial technique to free ourselves from our worries. Whenever we can observe a problem from a fresh perspective, our hardship won't seem too difficult.

If there is nothing in the world that can give you relief, create something of your own.

Replace laziness with self-motivation

Sometimes, I don't feel like doing anything. I just feel I need a break so that I can simply enjoy my life. In such cases, I always remind myself about my wish of becoming an extraordinary person. Everyone reads quotes and inspiring messages, but when it comes to applying them, we rarely recall them. Listen to yourself while reminding yourselves of various life lessons. Motivate yourself to make each new day better than yesterday.

Extraordinary people do things even when they don't feel like doing them. They know that practicing their art will always make them feel better.

Convert negativity to optimism

Many times, I've seen people speak negative words like "I don't deserve to be loved", "everyone hates me", "I'm very bored", "I'm not made for good things", or "I'm always stuck in darkness" etc. When we speak negative to ourselves, our subconscious mind slowly starts attracting only negative things. To attract positive things, it's important to first realize that we are very much deserving of them. There are so many good things out there, but we rarely choose to observe them. We can drive inspiration from every little thing out there. We just need to expand our vision and the way we receive things.

Never speak negative things to yourself. Stay positive and have faith in the goodness out there.

Allow yourself to heal

I never understand the reason behind certain things. Some incidents like 'loss of a loved one' leave us with unbearable pain. Everyone says time heals every wound, but I think, with time, we simply learn how to manage our pain better. Some incidents never fade from our memory, no matter how hard we try. We just slowly learn new ways to cope up. One thing that we can keep reminding ourselves very often is that life is too short and fragile. This can help us realize that we should keep expressing ourselves, spread love, and never hold grudges.

It's not always necessary to know the reason behind certain things. Some things sure go wrong in our journey of life; what's more important is that we allow ourselves to heal from the hurt.

Importance of self-care

There are times when we feel like nobody cares for what we are going through. We all know that a child cries when he needs care. He cannot express his feelings by speech and so, he'll make tantrums. On the other hand, adults can convey how they feel and so, they should never hesitate to ask for help. Unless we tell someone how we feel, others won't understand. Asking for help is bravery because that way, you put faith in another person.

Whenever someone does something wrong to me, I often end up forgiving people, thinking that, after all, they belong from my country. Feelings of patriotism and unity should be enough for a person to love their nation in an unbiased way.

Nobody knows your problems better than you. Be kind enough to handle yourself with all the care you need. Believe that you have the power required to face the challenges life has to put in front of you. You may take help/support to figure things out, but always remember the fact that the sun shines alone in the whole sky and still holds the power to brighten up the whole city.

Embrace the beauty of differences

Many times in my life, I have felt like there are so many differences between me and my friends, but then I discovered a fresh perspective so that I could embrace the beauty that any kind of relationship gives us. The perspective is that, instead of searching differences in each other, we must explore our similarities together, because that opens more doors for love and acceptance in our lives. I always try my best to be a giver when it comes to sharing love with my loved ones. I push myself to give more than I receive. My uncle once taught me, that life is to give, not to take.

Respect all sorts of differences; embrace their beauty, flourish through them. They are the very reasons you can get a chance to grow seeds of love in your relationships.

Challenges are opportunities for growth

At some point, we all think there are too many problems in our life. We get frustrated, and start thinking why do we even have to face so much hardship. Don't you think we should look at our challenges from a different viewpoint so as to lessen their burden? Different perspectives allow us to expand our horizons and think in an open-minded way. I think we should not fear our obstacles, because they are the very reasons that allow us to learn new things and grow. Also, it's always easy to remember the lessons we learn from our mistakes.

Don't lament that there are too many difficult situations, instead, find solutions one by one.

Don't ask life to take away all your problems. Instead, ask it to give you a set of good problems that can strengthen your soul.

Be your own hero

There are times when I feel very low and don't know what to do. In such situations, there's only one thing that saves me; perspective shift. If I get negative thoughts, I intentionally start thinking positive and empowering thoughts so that they can calm my mind. Whenever I feel like there should be someone who should care for our happiness, I explain myself that we can always be our own hero. We can achieve anything that we put our mind to, if we can realize how blessed we are with all the things that have been provided to us by life.

Try to keep yourself most inspired/motivated in the times you feel low. It's how you bring a positive change in your life. Don't wait for anyone to come and make you happy, be that person for yourself.

Are you listening to your needs or desires?

At some point, everyone feels like they are not getting the many things that they want in their life. In such situations, what one can do is question themselves and ask how many desires are enough in order to become happy. Once one wish is fulfilled, we start wishing for other things. This makes us materialistic. Our parents have given us such a beautiful life that we should feel blessed for every tiny bit provided to us. This would definitely help us to realize that all our needs are often met even before we ask for them.

Your desires satisfy your ego. Always ask yourself whether you are listening to your needs or your desires.

Forgive yourself for your past mistakes

Sometimes I feel like I am unable to forget the mistakes I made in my past. My mistakes haunt me again and again, but before they overpower me, I shift my thought pattern. I explain myself to focus on the lessons learned from them. I also explain myself that it's completely alright to forgive ourselves as quickly as we forgive everyone else. One can always try to develop a habit of dealing with their hardships with grace, as grace and growth go hand in hand.

Forgive yourself for your past mistakes. Be thankful for all the lessons and learning from those mistakes. Always look up and keep moving forward in life.

Why comparison and competition is bad

Sometimes I feel like others are doing so much better than me in their life. The truth is, comparison and competition destroy us. That's why I remind myself again and again that the only person we should compare ourselves with is the person we were yesterday. We can surely take inspiration from lives of other people but questioning our own worth is wrong in every way. Self-doubt only limits us from achieving great things. What you believe you deserve, you achieve.

Comparing your journey to that of others will only lower your confidence. Remember that you are where you are today because of all the decisions you made in your life, and so, be happy with what all you have accomplished while working for changes that prove to be better for your future.

Turn loneliness to feeling peace

There are times when we feel lonely and helpless in life. In such times, we often start blaming other people for leaving us alone or for not staying by our side when we need them. This perception further delays our blessings as we do not embrace what lies in front of us. Instead of criticizing others, we should try to solve our problem. Sometimes, isolation is good, as it allows us to self-reflect and become more empathetic. In addition, we can give time to ourselves to practice new activities. Maybe this could help us discover new passion.

Isolation stimulates the creative mind. You can always try some mental exercise for activities which involve creativity of mind.

Live your best life

Sometimes, I feel lazy and don't want to do anything except watching T.V, but then I explain to myself that time is precious and should be used wisely. You only live once, and so, it's important to understand the importance of every passing minute.

Take one day at a time and live each day to the fullest. Every new day, remind yourself that today is a good day to do something great, and see how your life elevates to the ultimate heights of happiness. Accomplishing even small tasks can be beneficial for the release of happiness hormones (dopamine and serotonin) in our brain.

The actions you take every moment are creating your story. Make sure you live your best life.

Feel grateful for negative experiences

I feel like I've been through, and still facing so many negative experiences in my life, but then I look at them as opportunities for growth and feel grateful that they make me physically, emotionally and mentally strong. I believe we should embrace the good and endure through the bad. Practicing this habit helps us to enhance the values of patience and discipline. Patience further helps an individual to enhance the quality of self-control, which ultimately helps to boost self-confidence.

Never give up on the attitude of growth mindset. One day, life will definitely give you the fruits of your patience, either in the form of blessings or a lesson.

Stay flexible with your lifestyle

At some point, everyone feels like their life is very monotonous and unexciting. Whenever I get such kind of feeling, I change the order of the tasks that I perform in my daily routine. Even small changes can make things seem different. Assign yourself new tasks every day so as to gain more wisdom. Try to dedicate some time to a creative hobby. Be in a healthy competition with yourself to make your life exciting and fulfilling.

Always remember that it's very important to stay flexible with our lifestyle, as being too strict can affect our mental health in negative ways.

Whenever you have to make some changes in your life (or lifestyle habits), remember you need to be extra patient with yourself because good things always take time to incorporate/absorb.

Don't let others burn your blood

Sometimes, I think why people mistreat us. But then I believe why should we give such people power over oneself. A quote by Mahatma Gandhi which says "nobody can hurt you without your permission" has helped me a lot in my life. We often allow others to affect our thought process by thinking about their bad words or actions over and over again. Others behave a certain way because of their own worries, and so, we must never let them spoil our calm state of mind. Also, one can always set healthy boundaries when it comes to allowing interference from others.

Never let misbehaviour of others affect your peace.
Their actions are only a reflection of their character.
Don't let them burn your blood.

Don't wait for validation or motivation

Have you ever felt the need for motivation in your life? At some point, we all feel like we need to hear some motivating words to push ourselves for work. It's good if we realize that we need some inspiration or a sense of purpose that can drive us forward in life, but it's best if we are disciplined enough to realize how capable we already are. Take responsibilities and you'll automatically become disciplined. This way, you will also be able to eliminate the need for any external motivating factor.

Unless we try to perform, we cannot succeed.

Don't wait for validation or motivation to take the next step; one day you'll be proud of yourself for being an unstoppable spirit.

Advancement is key

Sometimes I wonder why it is so tough to bring change, but lately I realized that it's because people believe in their beliefs in very stubborn ways. Everyone has been following some traditions from their past, and so, people find it difficult to rid themselves from old thinking patterns. When an elder puts their opinion in front of us, we must try to understand that they have been conditioned to think a particular way. Instead of questioning them, we can politely explain them the difference between right and wrong. To conclude, we all must realize how essential it is to keep ourselves updated with new things in this fast-changing world.

Most of the times, what matters to bring about a change is how many lives we can touch, how many lives we can influence in positive ways, and in how many lives we can make an impact that proves to be helpful for individuals.

Forget stress and do things with fun

While working for a goal, like weight loss, I keep feeling like I can't see any change even after working so hard. This makes me worry unless I explain myself that some goals need a little extra patience and enthusiasm. We should do things with fun and focus on the process, more than thinking about the goal.

Anxiety or worry simply takes our happiness away from us. We often forget to keep ourselves happy while working towards achieving our dreams. We keep waiting for a particular moment to arrive so that it can bring us happiness. However, it is equally amazing to stay happy during the process.

Don't stress over anything in life because it only takes your happiness away from you. Feel and do things with your heart immersed in them. Little changes bring huge improvement with time.

How to keep faith in tough times

I often wondered how a person can keep faith in tough times until I discovered a perspective that goes like "no matter how tough life gets, believe that good days will come". Whenever you feel low or lost, try to recall happy memories, take time to understand your feelings, remind yourself that you always have the power to choose your mood and be kind to yourself.

During your rough phase, hold onto your strengths and believe more in yourself to provide yourself the necessary support needed to heal your heart and soul.

Maturity is when you take little steps to keep yourself happy every-time you feel lost.

How to deal with mixed emotions

I often feel stuck with mixed emotions, but then I choose to observe my feelings and acknowledge my emotions. I try to share my feelings with a friend and automatically start feeling better. I explain myself to accept life as it unfolds every moment, because acceptance of circumstances can help a person challenge their own limits of tolerance.

Remember, when there's some emotion inside you, it's always trying to teach you something. So, keep focusing on the lessons life teaches you and it will help you grow beyond limits.

See one perspective beyond your present situation whenever you feel stuck due to your emotions. This will definitely save you from getting lost.

Stop blaming the system

At some point, everyone feels like they have never-ending problems in their life. Also, when we are unable to find solutions to those problems, we start blaming others and speak negative words, like "nobody understands" me. Instead, we should try to understand that problems provide us a golden chance to push our creative boundaries. Instead of blaming the system, we should choose to find a way. We should push ourselves to discover new possibilities every-time we feel like there's no way out.

Don't let the storms/problems in your life break you.

Let them make you.

Get comfortable with the uncomfortable

There are times when we fear change, can't stay happy, or our emotions leave us emotionally drained. In such situations, we should take a break and distract ourselves with all the right kind of things that can help us enhance our creativity and conquer our fears.

Don't cry over petty things. If a situation challenges your beliefs, understand that life is trying to teach you something.

Don't fear change as and when required; be wiser and less wrong every new day. At frequent intervals, stay out of your comfort zone so that you can discover what makes you most happy.

Make unfamiliar familiar, get comfortable with the uncomfortable, and see your life shifting its dimension to the highest form of happiness.

How to make your dreams come true

Do you ever sit and wonder that there's so much work to do and feel confused about where to begin? In such cases, you can always try one method in which you just need to take one step in the present moment and not worry about the rest. Continue to practice this method unless you reach your goal. From thinking and dreaming about it to start taking action, it makes all the difference.

Start now, start small, but start. Make increments every day. All the efforts will add up one day and you'll look back and be proud of yourself that you believed in your ideas more than anyone. If nothing, at least you'll have tried pursuing your passion and not given up on what you really love doing.

Feed faith instead of fear

Have you ever wondered why people hurt us? In such cases, always remember that life is what we take it to be. Feed faith instead of fear and choose to look good in people. Don't complain that everyone hurts you; instead, try to understand that you can always use your pain for growth. Moreover, sometimes, we should try to look at things from other people's point of view; it helps us to respond better.

You are what you are today because of all the things you went through. Have no grudges, no regrets (be unapologetic), no complaints, and no demands.

Value your hardwork

While trying new things in life, we often feel "what if I fail?" A little shift in perspective can surely help us here. When failure comes, think how it can help you grow, how you can learn from it, how you can find the hidden lessons, and not just lament over it. Take chances rather than regretting later.

Set you benchmark high. Your potential will automatically push you to overcome every setback and achieve big goals.

Measure your success by how much you try and how much efforts you take, not by how good you perform. Value your hardwork.

There are many instances in life where we cannot change the situation. In such cases, we should choose to change our response towards the problems. For example, if you get a lot of thoughts, you can always channelize them to increase your imagination power. Let's consider an example where you feel like why do our parents keep checking up on us. Here, you can shift your perspective to think that, maybe, they get happy by seeing us happy. Let's see one more example. When things don't go our way, we often blame our upbringing. Instead, we should feel blessed that it gave us a certain uniqueness that sets us apart from the crowd today.

Always look at the bigger picture and bright side of things for a happy life. Also, you can always choose to use negative situations to build strength in you.

Life will pull you into dark situations again and again, but remember that it's always your choice if you wish to light a candle. Perspective shift helps us to find light even in the darkest of times and takes care of our happiness even when we have to face the most difficult journey.

ABOUT THE AUTHOR

Nitu Ramchandani is a warm-hearted personality. She believes that goodwill is the purest form of love. She is always inspired by teachings and words of Madhuri Dixit, a great idol and a huge inspiration.

Nitu loves simple living and high thinking. When her experiences married her research, she found interest in expressing her thoughts and emotions through different writings. It's her dream to become a great writer, poet, and author. Nitu loves to explore various things, things that can add meaning to her life. Her previous books are "Infinite Delight" (first book) and "A light in every direction" (second book).

You may connect with Nitu through her Facebook page -

Library of a poet (facebook.com/Libraryofapoet)

or Instagram page

(https://instagram.com/libraryofawriter).